Exit 8

Jennifer Degenhardt & Diego Ojeda

For all who make the journey.

TABLE OF CONTENTS

ACKNOWLEDGEMENTS

Special thanks to Isaías, a real person and friend of one of the authors, who recently made the journey to the United States and who, in part, inspired this story.

AUTHORS' NOTE

There are as many reasons that people leave their home countries to emigrate to others, perhaps as many reasons as there are humans who migrate. The push-pull factors surrounding human migration is often only viewed through a political lens. Through this story, we welcome readers to see immigrants as people first.

ii

Chapter 1
The Arrival

"We are here," Humberto tells me.

We walk into the apartment. The apartment is not very big.

There are six men in the apartment.

"Hey, everyone. I am Isaías."

The men speak to me:

"Hi, Isaías. My name is David. I am from El Salvador.

"Welcome. I am Salvadoran too. My name is José."

"Hi," says another man. "My name is Igor. I am Nicaraguan."

"My name is Nicolás."

"My name is Ronaldo. I am Honduran."

"Hello. My name is Jesús. I am from Ecuador.

There are many men and many new names.

"Are you hungry?" Humberto asks me.

"No, I am not hungry, but I am thirsty," I tell him.

David says, "We have water."

"Thank you," I say to him.

I am very sleepy. I want to sleep.

The trip to the United States is long and hard. I need to sleep.

Humberto gives me the water.

"Here you go, Isaías. Welcome."

"Thank you, my friend. I am very sleepy."

"You need to sleep. Very early tomorrow morning we are going to Exit 8 to look for work."

Exit 8?

I want to ask Humberto, but I am very sleepy.

Tomorrow...

Tomorrow I will ask for more information.

Hello!

Glad we caught you...

We wanted to let you know about the poems that you'll find at the end of each chapter. They are poems written by the main character. He likes to write and wants to share more of his thoughts with you through his poetry.

Enjoy!

The Arrival

I am here
I am tired
Where am I?

I want to rest
I want to sleep
I want to dream.

I have questions
I am thirsty
I have dreams,
I want to imagine a better future.

Chapter 2
Work?

It is morning, but it is dark outside.

"Let's go, Isaías," Humberto says to me.

"I am coming," I say.

It is four-thirty in the morning. It is dark and it is cold.

"Where...? I ask Humberto.

"We are going to Exit 8."

"What is Exit 8?" I ask him.

"It is a place to look for work."

I am afraid. Everything is new.

Humberto, three other men and I go to Exit 8.

*****

We arrive at Exit 8.

There are other men there.

Exit 8 is off the highway.

"Good morning, Rafael. Good morning, Pepe," Humberto says to them. "I want to introduce you to Isaías. He is from my hometown."

"Good morning, Isaías. My name is Rafael. I am from Colombia.

"Hello. I am Pepe. I am Mexican."

"Hello," I say to them. "I am Isaías."

"Are you here for work?" Pepe asks me.

"Yes. You're right. I am here to work – for my family in my country," I say to him.

"We are, too."

I am young. I am 26 years old. I am young. the journey to the United States is hard for everyone, especially older people.

"I am 53 years old," Pepe tells me. I am lucky to be here. I have been in this country for four years."

I want to ask him more information, but Humberto says, "This place, Exit 8, is a place to look for work. The people who need workers come here and offer us work."

"And is there work?" I ask him.

"Some days, yes. Other days, no," Humberto tells me.
We are at Exit 8 all day. There is no work today. It is cold.

I am hungry and I am thirsty.

Everything is new. It is hard for me.

EXIT 8

It is morning
But it is not sunny.
It is cold outside
But my heart is frozen.

The exit on the highway
is the entrance to a new life.
My name is Isaías,
and it does not matter if it is
Monday or Friday,
in this country
I just want to work.

Chapter 3
Memories

I am alone in the apartment. The other men are not here.

I take out the photo of my family and I look at it. The photo is old, but it is my favorite photo. It is a photo of my wife and daughters at home.

My wife's name is Amalia.
She is pretty. She has brown eyes and brown hair. Her hair is long.
I love my wife.
I love her. A lot.
My daughters' names are Maricela and Juanita.
Maricela is nine (9) years old, and Juanita is three (3) years old.
I love my daughters. I love them. A lot.

Why am I here? Why am I not with my family?

I am in the United States because there is more work here. There are more opportunities to work.

In my country there are many things. There are plants, many fruits, and many beautiful places. But there is no work. There is not enough work for everyone. There is no work, and it is hard to live without money.

I have been here for seven (7) days.

I want to be home in my country. I want to be with my family. I want to talk to my wife. I want to talk to my daughters.

But that is not possible. It is impossible. I do not have a phone.

I am here now. I am in the United States to work. I want to work. I need to work a lot.

But I am not working. There is no work. I am not working yet.

There is no work in my country and no work here – for now.

But I am lucky. I am here. I got to the United States. Some people do not arrive because the journey is hard and dangerous. Some people die and others are deported.

I look at the photo. I like everything in the photo.

I like my wife's hair.
I like my daughters' eyes.
I like our house.
I like the ears and the nose of our dog.
I like the sounds of our town: the sounds of nature, the sounds of the people and the sounds of the animals.

I like my country a lot.

One day I want to return. I am going to return.

But first I need to work. I want to work.

Maybe tomorrow.

Seven Days

Seven days has the week, and
in the calendar of my heart,
each one adopted a name.

Monday is for Amalia, my love.
Tuesday is for little Juanita.
Wednesday is for Maricela, the
older one.

Thursday is for my parents.
Friday, for my brothers, it is.

Saturday is for my* close friends.
Sunday is for me,
as I prepare my heart
for a new week
so that every day I
I work with love.

Chapter 4
At Exit 8

It is cold.

It is very different from the weather in my country.

I am very cold here...

We are here at the Exit. We want to work. There are eight (8) men here. The other men are not cold because they have good clothes for the cold.

"Hola, Isaías," Pepe says to me. Pepe is the old guy in the group. "How are you?" he asks me.

"Good morning, Pepe. I am fine. And you? How are you?

"I am fine, thank you. Is there work today?" I ask him.

"Yes. You need to be positive," Pepe tells me.

At that moment a truck arrives. The man in the truck is United Statesian, but he speaks a little Spanish.

He says:

"*Necesito seis a trabajar a mi casa. Quiero igual hombres ayer[1].* (I need six to work at my house. I want the same men as yesterday)."

The other six men get in the truck.

_____

[1] quiero igual hombres ayer: quiero los mismos hombres que ayer. (I want the same men as yesterday.)

Pepe and I do not go with the group. We did not work yesterday.

Are we going to work today?

Yes. We are going to work today. I need to be positive.

The truck leaves. The group leaves us at Exit 8, Pepe and me. We are alone.

The truck leaves, and it leaves us alone.

I am a little sad, but Pepe is not sad. Pepe is very positive.

"Isaías, at the beginning... the United States is really hard. Really hard. A person is not with his family, and he is not in his country.

"Pepe, it is so hard. I am not with my family. I love my wife and my daughters," I tell him.

"Yes. You are here because you love your family. You want a better life for them, right?

"Yes. You are right," I tell him.

"I love my family. And I want to be with my family. I want to be with my wife and children, too," Pepe tells me.

"And why are you here, Pepe?" I ask him.

"Oh, Isaías. The situation is very hard in my country. It is not hard in your country?"

"Yes, it is. There is not a lot of work," I tell him.

"It is similar in my country. There is no work. And I have a farm, but there is no water for the plants."

It is very windy and cold. It is awful.

Pepe talks some more: "If there is no water, there are no plants. If there are no plants, there is no fruit. If there is no fruit, there is no work...and if there is not work..."

"It is an awful situation, Pepe. It is very hard," I tell him. "Awful, Pepe."

"I agree. I agree, Isaías," Pepe tells me.

"And is there enough work here?" I ask him.

"Yes. There is work," he tells me. "You need to be positive."

I want to work. I want to work because I want to pay the rent. I need to work for my family too.

I have a dream...a dream of a good life in my country...

But in this moment, another truck arrives. The man does not get out of the truck, and he does not speak Spanish:

"I need two guys," the man says. "I pay at the end of the day."

I do not speak English. I ask Pepe, "What is the man saying?"

"He has work. He pays at the end of the day."

Pepe talks to the man, "OK. We work."

We get in the truck with the man.

We are going to work.

Dreams

The cold is more intense
when there is no work.
The plants don't grow
without water.
I am sad
without hope.

Friends are like the sun.
They bring heat
in the winter.
They bring water
so the dream grows.

The dream is not to get money,
it is the warmth, the water,
the prosperity,
it is being able to sleep
and wake up happy.

In the United States I am,
but together with my family
lies my heart.

Chapter 5
Work!

We are in the truck. Pepe and I do not talk. And the man from here does not talk to us.

It is silent.

I am happy. I am going to work today. I am going to work for my family. Yes, I am happy.

*****

We arrive.

There are many other men. Some men are working. Others are talking.

The man from the truck says, "Those trees over there. You are going to cut them down and take them away."

I look at Pepe. Pepe says to me, "We are going to cut down the small trees."

"OK."

Pepe and I work a lot.
We work hard.

The trees aren't big, but there are a lot of trees.

We work the whole day.

It is late.

We work for nine (9) hours.

The work is hard.

After nine hours. We return to Exit 8 with the man.

The man leaves us there.

"*Gracias por la oportunidad de trabajar* (Thank you for the opportunity to work)," I say to the man.

"You pay us?" Pepe asks.

The man takes out the money.

He gives us each forty (40) dollars.

Pepe is not happy. "Sir, we worked all day. All day. This is not enough."

The man says "sorry" and leaves in his truck.

I am sad. I work a lot, but I do not earn a lot.

No, I am not happy. I am sad.

Trees

I'm ready!
I come to work
You want me to cut trees,
and for that you will pay me.

I don't know how to cut a tree,
I only like to plant
But here I come to work
and nothing to ask.

You want me to cut thirty (30)
trees
and I think it will take me eight (8)
hours.
It doesn't matter, it's okay.
For my family, I can work without
stopping twenty-four (24) hours.

My father taught me
That any work is dignified.
The whole day I will work,
Well, with dignity,
each dollar I will earn.

Chapter 6
Exit 8

I am alone this morning at Exit 8.

It is early.

I am looking for other work.

I want a different job than the one from the other day. A similar job? No. No, thank you.

A man arrives. He gets out of the truck, and he shakes my hand.

"Hi, I am George. *Jorge. Mucho gusto* (Nice to meet you)," he tells me.

I have a huge smile on my face. George's Spanish is not very good, but I like it.

"*Hola, soy Isaías.*"

"Do you need a job, Isaías?" he asks me.

"Yes, sir. I need one. And I like to work."

"Bueno. Bueno. *¿Tú vas con mí?* (You go with me?)," he asks me.

I like George. I like to work. I need the money. I want the money. I need to send the money to my family, but...

"How much do you pay?" I ask him.

George says, "I pay *bueno*, Isaías. Ten (10) dollars an hour. Is that good?

"Yes, sir. That's very good. Thank you."

I go with George in his truck.

*****

We arrive at a big house, a very big house.

The house is not in the city, it is in the suburbs.

I have so many questions.

Is it a private house?

Who lives here?

Why do they have a very big house?

"Let's go, Isaías," George says. "I will introduce you to the other workers."

Like the other day, there are many men there. Everyone is working. There are some Hispanic people here. I am happy. Do they speak Spanish?

George introduces me to the group in Spanish:

"Hombres, es Isaías. Él gusta trabajar[2]. Trabajar con ustedes[3] (Guys, this is Isaías. He likes to work. He will work with you." says George.

Everyone says "hello" and "welcome."

A man says to me, "Isaías, you are going to work with us ¿OK?"

"Great," I tell him. "Thank you."

"If you need water, there's water over there," the other guy says.

I am happy. George is good. And the workers are good too. It is a good place to work.

We work all day. When we are hungry and we are thirsty, we do not work for a time. All the men talk a lot. They are good. They are not bad.

---

[2] él gusta trabajar: le gusta trabajar.
[3] trabajar con ustedes: él trabaja con ustedes.

During the time that we are not working, an official arrives at the house. A businessman? He has on formal clothes. He talks to George first, and he speaks to him in English.

After a few minutes, the man speaks with us:

"Hola, hombres. ¿Cómo están ustedes? (Hi, guys. How are you?)

What? What??

How...?

The official speaks Spanish? Yes, the official speaks Spanish. Why?

The workers talk with him.

"Hello, Mr. Goodman. How are you?"

The official, Mr. Goodman, is very good too. He says to us, "You guys are doing a good job here. It is going to be a great community center. Thank you for your work."

I have so many questions.

"Who is he?" I ask another worker.

"He is a government representative. He is a representative in Washington D.C.," he tells me.

"I need to go," I tell him. "I do not have documents."

"No. It is okay. Mr. Goodman works with a government program that works with undocumented people. He's a good guy."

Mr. Goodman talks to me and shakes my hand. "Hi, I am Jamey Goodman. What is your name?"

"My name is Isaías. Nice to meet you, sir."

"Nice to meet you," he says to me. "Thank you for your work here."

"Sir, excuse me. How do you speak Spanish?" I ask him.

"I lived in Latin America for many years. I like the Latin American culture and I like Spanish," he tells me with a smile.

"How interesting," I tell him.

"This community center is very important. It is a center for all the undocumented persons in the region."

Impressive. This Mr. Goodman is interesting, intelligent and he likes people.

At the end of the day, George speaks to me:

"Isaías, a good day of work. How many hours?"

"Eight hours, sir."

"Here is eighty (80) dollars. You're a good worker. Do you want to return tomorrow?

"Yes, sir. I like the job. I am going to return tomorrow. Thank you."

"See you tomorrow, Isaías."

A New Opportunity

It is a new day
and at the new job
everyone welcomes me.

It is a new day
and today the trees I will not cut.
Today the sun is happy
and on the men's faces you can
see its smile.

The sun is happy
because a community center
we will build
with our hands.

Today is a new day
and in Spanish and in English
only happiness is heard.

Chapter 7
In the Apartment

I am in the apartment. There are many men in the apartment too.

"Hi, Isaías. How are you?" asks Humberto. "And the job?"

"Hi, Humberto. I am fine, thank you. The job is very good. I am going to return tomorrow."

"That's great, man. And they pay you well?" Humberto asks me.

"Yes. I am lucky. They pay me ten (10) dollars an hour," I tell him.

"That's great, man. Congratulations!" Humberto says.

I am happy. I want to talk with my wife, but it is not possible yet. I need more money so I can buy a phone.

And I am going to send money to my family.

Humberto talks to me again:

"Isaías, we are going to a Latino restaurant. Do you want to go with us?

"Yes. Thank you. I want to go. I am hungry, and I need to eat.

"We are going in thirty (30) minutes.

"That's great. Thank you."

Today is the beginning. Today is the beginning of my dream. I want my dream of earning money to come true. I want to send money to my family.

A Good Job

The apartment is not cold anymore.
The new job gives me strength,
it gives me vigor.

My name is no longer "the new guy."
My name is Isaías
and everyone knows who I am.

When the work is good
when they pay you well
it is easier to smile,
it is easier to dream.

Tomorrow with Mr. George
I am going to work.
From Monday to Saturday
all the money
for my family I will save.

Chapter 8
Going to the Supermarket

It is Sunday. I am in the apartment.

I work these days: Mondays, Tuesdays, Wednesdays, Thursdays, Fridays, and Saturdays.

I do not work on Sundays.

I work a lot every month. I work six (6) days of the week, eight (8) hours a day.

The community center in the big house needs a lot of work. The center is going to be ready in a year.

I like the job a lot. I like the workers too.

And working at the future community center gives me a good idea...

But first, I need to go the supermarket. In the supermarket there is a bank. At the bank I am going to send money to my family.

It is sunny today, but it is cold, and it is windy. I leave the apartment and I walk to the supermarket alone.

*****

In the supermarket I am alone. I am not with any of the other men, David, José, Igor, Nicolás, Ronaldo or Jesús.

I am not afraid, but I am nervous. Sending the money is very important.

I go to the part of the supermarket where the bank is.

I talk to a woman. She works at the bank.

"How can I help you?" she asks me in English.

What is she saying?

I am very nervous. It is very important to send the money, but I do not speak English.

I speak to her in Spanish.

"*Buenos días. Quiero mandar dinero a mi familia en mi país* (Good morning. I want to send money to my family in my country)," I say to the woman.

"Do you speak English?" she asks me.

"*Quiero mandar dinero a mi familia*," I say to her.

"I do not understand what you want. And Lucia is not here yet. I can't help you. You will need to come back," she says to me.

I take out the money.

"Este dinero. Quiero mandar a mi familia (This money. I want to send to my family)," I say to her.

I give her the money.

"No. I can't take that. Mister, I can't help you. I do not know what you want, and Lucia is not here to translate. You need to come back."

The woman tells me "NO". What do I do?

I am frustrated.

I am angry.

I need to send the money. But I do not speak English. This situation is awful for me.

I have been in the United States for two months and my family does not have money.

Frustrated and angry, I return to the apartment.

Two Languages

Today I am going to the bank
and to my family, money
I will send.

In my pocket
many days of work
in cash are there.

My heart wants to sing,
I'm happy because my family
I can help.

There's only one inconvenience
that English I cannot understand.
I don't know how to send the
money.

A little sad and frustrated
I return home with a new plan.
Starting tomorrow,
English I am going to learn.

Chapter 9
At the Workplace

It is Monday. It is the start of the week.

I am still frustrated by the experience in the bank. I have the money, but I cannot send it to my family.

But I am happy too. I have work and I have a job that pays well.

I am going to earn more money.

I am at the community center. I am with the other workers and with George too.

"Good morning, guys," says George. "We have a lot to do today. Two weeks to, uh...*completar trabajo* (finish the work)."

George's Spanish is not perfect. But George communicates with the workers.

"Let's go, Isaías. We need to work," says a friend.

"I am coming," I tell him.

If George speaks Spanish and it is not perfect... English for me...

Why is English so hard?

It is hard, but I need to speak English.

Yes, I want to return to my country one day, but I am in the United States now. And I want to communicate with other people here. I need to speak English.

During the afternoon, Mr. Goodman arrives to talk with George, and he talks with us too.

"Men, the work you are doing with this house for the community center is excellent. Thank you for all your work."

He's a good man Mr. Goodman.

"And men, there is going to be a public celebration for the new center open to everyone. I want to invite you. And, if I can help you, talk to me.

Mr. Goodman is going to leave, but I want to speak with him.

"Excuse me, Mr. Goodman," I say to him. "I have a question for you."

"Of course. What is your name again?" he asks me.

"My name is Isaías."

"Oh, yes. Thank you. My memory..."

"No problem, sir. I need some information," I say to him.

"How can I help," he tells me. "What information do you need?"

"I need to learn English," I tell him.

"That's a good idea, Isaías. Here's a number for you."

Mr. Goodman writes a number on a paper, and he gives it to me.

"This number is for a community center that has English classes for people who want to speak English."

"Great, thank you."

I am nervous...

"And the price for the classes?" I ask him. "I do not have a lot of extra money."

"The classes do not cost anything. They are part of a government program. They are free," he tells me.

"Excellent, Mr. Goodman. Thank you so much for the information," I tell him.

I am not frustrated. I am happy. I am going to speak English.

For the rest of the day, I have a big smile on my face.

English

I have a plan.
Today Mr. Goodman I will ask,
how to learn English
very fast.
I like Spanish
and with all of my friends here
I can communicate.

But I need English
if at the bank
I want to talk.
To send money to my family

I'm not from here
everything is new to me.
To speak English
in the United States
makes life easier.

Chapter 10
In English Class

After work one day, I walk to English class at the other community center. I am nervous, but I am happy.

I am going to the class with Humberto and David. They have been in the United States longer and they do not speak English. But they want to speak.

We talk:

"They tell me that English is very hard," says David.

"Everything is hard at the beginning," says Humberto.

"Yes. English is new and it is going to be hard at first," I tell them. "But we are going to speak. We need to be positive."

Next week is the celebration for the community center where I work. I want to introduce myself to the other people in English...

*****

In English class, there are many people from many countries. Everyone wants to speak English.

"Good evening class," the teacher says to us. "Welcome to English class. Tonight, we will learn how to introduce ourselves in English."

A woman who speaks a little English says to us, *"Buenas tardes, clase. Esta noche vamos a aprender a presentarnos en inglés."*

The teacher speaks:

"My name is Deirdre. I am from New York. I am from the United States."

The teacher writes the questions:

What is your name?
Where are you from?

OK. It is not hard. It is easy. I write in my notebook.

Everyone talks in English:

My name is Anna. I am from Democratic Republic of Congo. I am Congolese.

My name is Pierre. I am from Haiti. I am Haitian.

My name is Mahmoud. I am from Pakistan. I am Pakistani.

My name is David. I am from Colombia. I am Colombian.

My name is Humberto. I am from Guatemala. I am Guatemalan.

I introduce myself in English. It is not natural in the beginning, but I speak more and more. At the end of class, it is easier.

After a few classes I go to the bank. I am going to speak with the woman in English. I am going to send the money to my family.

I am happy. I am not frustrated. I am going to write a lot in my notebook.

Hello, my name is Isaías...

Hello again!

Glad we caught you...

We are hoping you have enjoyed the story so far. We wanted to remind you to turn the page for the poem for this chapter. Isaías has more to tell you.

Enjoy and thanks for reading!

My nombre is

Hello my friends,
Mi nombre no es Andrés,[*]
Me llamo Isaías[**]
and I can speak
en español y en inglés.

I came here
hace unos días [***]
y aunque fácil no es,[****]
now I'm very happy
porque puedo hablar inglés.[*****]

*Mi nombre no es Andrés: My name is not Andrés.
**Me llamo Isaías: My name is Isaías.
***hace unos días: some days ago.
****y aunque fácil no es: and though it is not easy.
*****porque puedo hablar inglés: because I can speak English.

Muchos amigos tengo

en este país.*

Cada uno de ellos**

their family left.

They came here

para un mejor futuro buscar.***

Si un día trabajando me ves****

Don't forget to shake my hand

que en mi puedes confiar.*****

---

*muchos amigos tengo en este país: I have many friends in this country.
**cada uno de ellos: every one of them.
***para un mejor futuro buscar: to look for a better future.
****si un día trabajando me ves: if you see me working one day.
***** que en mi puedes confiar: you can trust me.

ABOUT THE AUTHORS

Diego Ojeda

Diego Ojeda is a Spanish teacher in Louisville, Kentucky. Diego has written and published three CI poetry books and a short stories book. Diego is also an international Second Language Acquisition teacher trainer as well as a well-regarded teaching resources creator.

Diego shares most of his ideas and activities in his blog www.SrOjeda.com.

 @DiegoOjeda66

 @Sr_Ojeda

 www.youtube.com/c/DiegoOjedaEDU

www.srojeda.com
Other books by Diego Ojeda

Poetry:

Corazón sin borrador
Poems about interpersonal relationships at school.

Acuerdo natural
Poems about the environment and our commitment to Earth.

Nostalgia migrante
Poems about the human experience of migration.

Short stories

Sonrisas ocultas
12 short stories about returning to school during the COVID-19 pandemic.

Jennifer Degenhardt

Jennifer Degenhardt taught high school Spanish for over 20 years and now teaches at the college level. At the time she realized her own high school students, many of whom had learning challenges, acquired language best through stories, so she began to write ones that she thought would appeal to them. She has been writing ever since.

Other titles by Jen Degenhardt:

La chica nueva | *La Nouvelle Fille* | The New Girl | *Das Neue Mädchen* | *La nuova ragazza*
La chica nueva (the ancillary/workbook volume, Kindle book, audiobook)
Salida 8 | *Sortie no. 8* | Exit 8
Chuchotenango | *La terre des chiens errants* | *La vita dei cani*

Pesas | *Poids et haltères* | Weights and Dumbbells |*Pesi*

Luis, un soñador

El jersey | The Jersey | *Le Maillot*

La mochila | The Backpack | *Le sac à dos*

Moviendo montañas | *Déplacer les montagnes* | Moving Mountains | *Spostando montagne*

La vida es complicada | *La vie est compliquée* | Life is Complicated

La vida es complicada Practice & Questions (workbook)

El Mundial | *La Coupe du Monde* | The World Cup

Quince | Fifteen | *Douze ans*

Quince Practice & Questions (workbook)

El viaje difícil | *Un voyage difficile* | A Difficult Journey

La niñera

¡¿Fútbol...americano?! | *Football...américain ?!*

Era una chica nueva

Levantando pesas: un cuento en el pasado

Se movieron las montañas

Fue un viaje difícil

¿Qué pasó con el jersey?

Cuando se perdió la mochila

Con (un poco de) ayuda de mis amigos | With (a little) Help from My Friends | *Un petit coup de main amical* | *Con (un po') d'aiuto dai miei amici*

La última prueba | The Last Test

Los tres amigos | Three Friends | *Drei Freunde* | *Les trois amis*

La evolución musical

María María: un cuento de un huracán | María María: A Story of a Storm | *Maria Maria: un histoire d'un orage*

Debido a la tormenta | Because of the Storm

La lucha de la vida | The Fight of His Life

Secretos | *Secrets*

Como vuela la pelota

Cambios | *Changements* | Changes

De la oscuridad a la luz

El pueblo | The Town

84

@JenniferDegenh1

@jendegenhardt9

@PuentesLanguage &
World LanguageTeaching Stories (group)

Visit www.puenteslanguage.com to sign up to receive
information on new releases and other events.

Check out all titles as ebooks with audio on
www.digilangua.co.

Made in the USA
Monee, IL
06 May 2023